Mia's Week at
Camp Living Waters

What to expect at summer camp
Marcy Schaaf

Introduction:

Welcome to Camp Living Waters, a place where summer dreams come true and adventures are waiting just around the corner! Join Mia as she embarks on an unforgettable journey filled with laughter, friendship, and exciting new experiences. From swimming in the lake with her buddies to discovering the joys of horseback riding, every day at camp is a new chapter in her thrilling story. With the Golden Toilet Seat award up for grabs and the grand talent show on the horizon, Mia's summer is sure to be packed with fun and surprises. Grab your backpack and get ready for an adventure like no other at Camp Living Waters!

It was the first day of summer camp at Camp Living Waters, and the sun was shining brightly. Mia hopped off the bus with excitement. She couldn't wait to see what adventures awaited her.

Mia found out she was in Cabin Pine with her friends from last year. She met her counselor, Sarah, who was super friendly and full of energy.

The first thing Mia did was unpack and choose her bunk. She picked the top bunk, feeling like she was on top of the world.

Next, Mia headed to the camp store to fund her account. The shelves were lined with candy, and she bought some gummy worms, her favorite treat.

At the sign-up table, Mia learned about all the activities available. There was swimming, woodworking, leather crafts, cooking, nature walks, and so much more! Mia was especially excited about the horse riding lessons.

The bell rang, and everyone gathered around the flagpole for the camp song. **"Camp Living Waters, where dreams come true, adventures waiting just for you!"**

After breakfast, it was time for the first and second activities.

Mia chose swimming. She loved the
buddy system as she swam in the lake
with her new friend, Lily.

Every day, the cabins had inspections. The cleanest cabin was awarded the Golden Toilet Seat for the day. Cabin Pine won it twice.

During free time, the camp store opened. Mia enjoyed her gummy worms and chatted with her friends. The store was a fun place to hang out.

The third activity for Mia was music. She learned about the flute.

After lunch, it was mail call then quiet time. Everyone relaxed reading or writing letters home. Mia wrote to her parents about all the fun she was having.

The forth and fifth activities came next. Mia tried horse riding for the first time. She was nervous but loved riding the gentle horse named Star.

Mia learned how to brush Star's mane and feed her apples. She felt a special bond forming with Star.

When dinner was over, it was time for the talent show. Mia couldn't wait to see everyone's performances. Some kids sang, some danced, and others told jokes.

Mia and her friends did a funny tune that made everyone laugh. The audience clapped and cheered loudly for them.

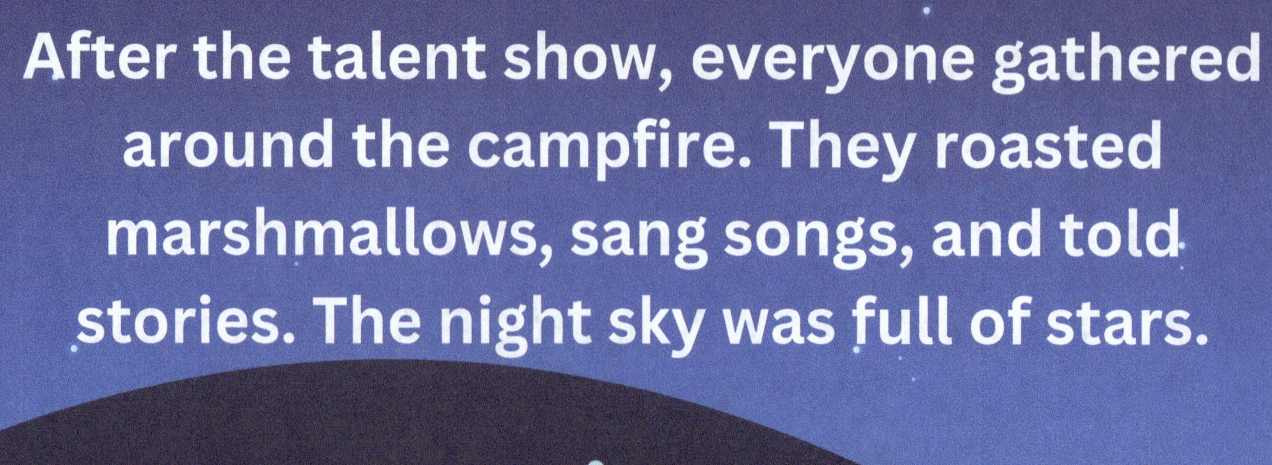

After the talent show, everyone gathered around the campfire. They roasted marshmallows, sang songs, and told stories. The night sky was full of stars.

Back in her bunk, Mia talk to her friends about the day's adventures. She couldn't wait to see what tomorrow would bring at Camp Living Waters.

The next morning, it was the same happy routine around the flagpole. Each day was filled with new activities and fun surprises.

Mia chose science and learned about planets!

In the afternoon, Mia couldn't wait to return to the stables. She learned how to saddle Star and practiced trotting around the paddock.

In art class, Mia and Kami made a
beautiful painting together.

The days flew by with so many activities.
Each night ended with the cozy campfire,
where everyone shared their favorite
moments of the day.

Mia loved spending time at the stables.
She learned how to clean the horses'
hooves and even helped with feeding
them hay and grain.

Sarah taught Mia and the other campers how to ride bareback. It was a bit tricky at first, but Mia soon got the hang of it.

The end of the week talent show was the highlight. This time, Mia performed a dance with some of her bunkmates, and they all wore matching costumes.

On the last day, they had a big feast. The dining hall was filled with laughter and stories from the week.

At the closing ceremony, each camper received a special badge. Mia got hers for horse riding. She felt so proud of her accomplishments.

Mia promised to write letters until next summer. It was hard to say goodbye, but she knew she'd be back next year.

As she boarded the bus home, Mia talked about all her favorite memories. Camp Living Waters had given her the best summer ever.

Mia looked out the window and waved goodbye to the camp. "See you next summer, Camp Living Waters!" she shouted.

She knew that next summer would bring even more fun and adventures. Camp Living Waters was her favorite place in the whole world.

She couldn't wait to tell her parents about the buddy swims, the crafts, the nature walks, and especially the horse riding adventures with Star.

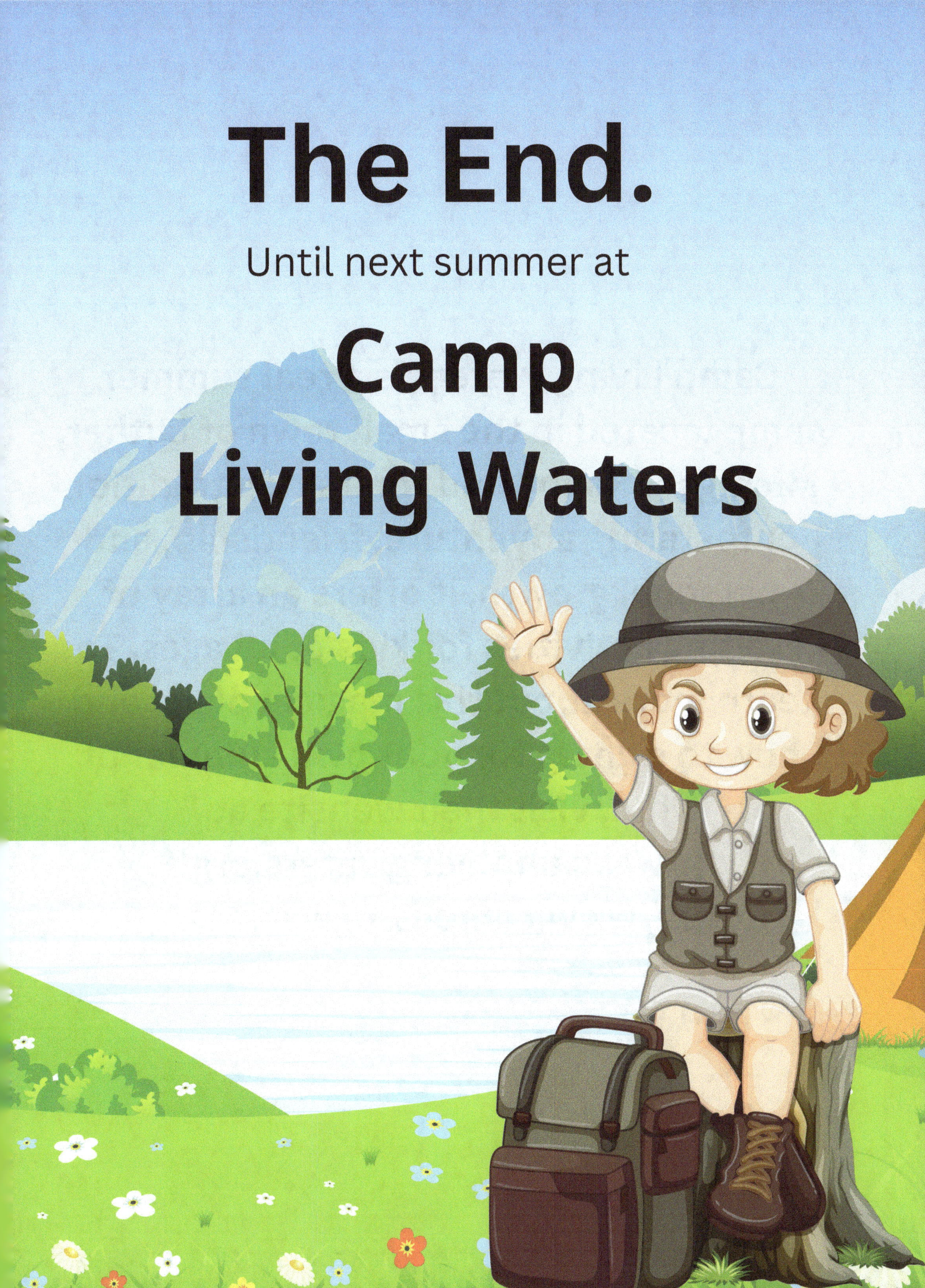

The End.
Until next summer at
Camp
Living Waters

Camp Living Waters is a real summer camp located in the small town of Luther, Michigan. Renowned for its rich tradition of fostering adventure, friendship, and personal growth, it offers an array of exciting activities for kids of all ages. To learn more about this magical place and how to sign up for your own summer of fun, visit their website at www.camplivingwaters.org.

Welcome to Camp Living Waters!

Nestled in the heart of Luther, Michigan, Camp Living Waters is the ultimate summer destination for kids seeking adventure, friendship, and unforgettable memories. Join Mia as she dives into a whirlwind of fun-filled activities, from swimming in the crystal-clear lake to mastering the art of horseback riding. Each day is a new opportunity for excitement, whether it's winning the coveted Golden Toilet Seat for the cleanest cabin, crafting unique leather creations, or showcasing talents at the end-of-week show.

This charming tale captures the essence of summer camp magic, where every sunrise brings the promise of new adventures and every sunset wraps up another perfect day. "Mia's Whirlwind Adventures at Camp Living Waters" is a heartwarming story that celebrates the joys of summer, the bonds of friendship, and the spirit of exploration. Join us at Camp Living Waters, where dreams come true and memories last a lifetime.

Books By Schaaf

www.BookBySchaaf.com

Find us at: